Gospel of the Dark Orisha

By
Edward Bruce Bynum

GOSPEL OF THE DARK ORISHA

EDWARD BRUCE BYNUM

Cover design by Cara Finch
www.cfinchart.com

Printed in the United States of America

ISBN 978-1945476-38-8

The Brutal Swan Press
PO Box 3121
Amherst, Massachusetts
01004

Dedicated to

William Boylin, Ernest Stableford, Jake Lesswing, Kenneth Bynum, Anthony Bynum, Irv Rhodes, Bennett Gaev, Bradford Cook, Josh Kroner, Charlie Bodhi, Ezra Sage Bynum, Elijah Jordan Bynum, John Morgan, Richard Hadley, Pierre Rouzier, John Higginson, George Foreman, Lee Lewis, Steve Hickman, Herb Gilmore, Bob Steinberg, Blake, Myles, Anton and Andre Bynum and the trailing memory of my father, my grandfathers and my great great great grandfathers, all of whose male force helps propel me through the world.

By the same author:

Poetry

> The Dreaming Skull
> GODZILLANANDA: His Life & Visions
> The First Bird: Songs of the Dark Body in Flight
> The Luminous Heretic
> The Magdalene Poems: The Love Letters of Jesus the Christ and Mary
> Magdalene
> TRANSMIGRATION: A Play for Voices
> Chronicles of the Pig & Other Delusions (Winner of the 2010
> Naomi Long Madgett Poetry prize)

Psychology/Psychiatry:

> The Family Unconscious: An Invisible Bond
> The Dreamlife of Families
> The Roots of Transcendence
> The African Unconscious: Roots of Ancient Mysticism and Modern
> Psychology
> Why Darkness Matters
> Legacy: Portrait of an Ancestor
> Dark Light Consciousness: Melanin, Serpent Power and the
> Luminous Matrix of Reality

Table of Contents

Acknowledgements:

Some of these poems have appeared in the following journals and periodicals; *"Standing Before the Sea After Jogging,"* Obsidian: Literature in the African Diaspora; *"A Woman is Walking* 1,2,3" The Worcester Review; *"Monday Evening,"* Connecticut River Review; *"Nephilim,"* Nefarious Ballerina; *"The Dark Religions Flying," "Remember Me #2,"* Valley Voices *" There Is a Bird Inside the Body that Flies with Us,"* Psych Discourse, *"Forms of a Woman,"* SILKWORM.

"In every corner of my soul is an altar to a different god."

Fernando Pessoa, 1888-1935

Gospel of the Dark Orisha

For Ernest M. Stableford
il miglior fabbro

"Consume my heart away; sick with desire
And fastened to a dying animal
It knows not what it is; and gather me
Into the artifice of eternity."
        Sailing To Byzantium, W.B.Yeats

I. *Walking Beside the Sea with Olokun*

I know the orgy of stones here,
This isle and inlet ill with birds.
Gulls watch over a dark Sabbath.

The summer-drunk weather
Multiplies umbrellas, children, mussels and havoc;
Young nuns escaped from the convent upriver.

They come to wash themselves in water
Flushed and full
Like Spring antelope,

Ears listening to the waves, migrating salmon, scanning the beach
For the wildebeests of the sand.
Offshore clouds, animal-shaped and religious,

Bash the air. Blooming, bending,
Stretching the sinews of time and space,
They extend out over reefs and whitecaps,

Sun bathers, sinners without names,
Expired salt oozing from them as from a dead whale's eye.
I hear my heartbeat in the thin sky,

Voweled, examined, fragmented and unafraid.
My extinguished heat flows upward in a dreamed apparition
One wave, one reality beyond my reach. I flow

Into broken water, into the warm ocean of Olokun.
This is bedrock, the deeper root surrounded
With element, stationary for uncountable months.

The sun breaks through in a giblet of color,
Raging orange, then scarlet, then subdued bone-white.
O I have breathed here billions of times

Crawled up from sandworm to shape-shifting shark.
I move amid sleek fleets of fish swimming through brain coral.
Reefs with green flowing sea hair

Get caught in my agitated teeth.
I take to the air in wings,
Ba bird freshly arisen from sleep, from the dead.

Torn out from the body's stiffening rack of meat
I rise, stare at the delirium my age,
My heat, my heartbeat has released.

Finally comfortable with defeat, the endless atoms
Of my failures, I run, empty myself,
Realign my soul with forgotten tongues

In the orbit of stars, the constellations my birth date holds
When I ruptured onto this living beach of conscious
Burning human fires.

Sirius and the dark companion stars the Dogon reach
With spirit eyes, disciplines of stone,
Streak by in the soul's flight

Back to the oval planets, the huge celestial vaginas,
The rings of dark matter,
The uterus of stars *before* the drama of matter.

Angels impervious to psychoanalysis
Come out, take my arms, lead
Through the gateway of waves, pulsations,

Contours, curves and canals of space
Gliding from one dimension into another.
My ghost and eyes feel heavy.

A blizzard of light and infinitesimal gyrations draws near;
Womb bags, Indian-head nickels, narratives
Between the serpents and birds

On their union again in the forest of bridges occurs
Leading legions of souls from the cannibal lairs
And vampire pits to resonance,

To travel through wormholes between the stars.
Avatars we are of light, sperm cast
Ages ago into the thighs of women.

I have learned to control my deaths,
Remain conscious through turrets
Of sleep, wish rooms and desires,

Pierce the organ bags of lives
Lived from the seas of Lemuria,
Alexandria, the chalcedony

And limestone temples of Thoth,
Horus, the three pyramids reflecting the belt of Orion
On earth the priests walked through

Opening the canal in the skull
Where the serpent slides through renewing
The dark initiations, the blood-purifying baths

Every awakened inner eye views.
Comfort, no substitute for health,
When beauty is sacrificed on the altar of wealth;

Shadows in the mirror of identity,
Diagnosis masquerading as a sense of self.
I approach the guardian of the first gate after death.

II. *The Remembering*

Earth self-immolates
Into bronze and gold, races of leaves
Expire to the ground, furnaces reopen,

Dreams of hibernation return to the bears.
In autumn the world prepares to starve itself down
To bone and ash.

I am reduced down, cast into the vestigial eye
Of my own self-image,a pomegranate seed
Roiling from room to room

Honeycombed with runes, memories
Of the sacred hour I return to again.
The muscle of spirit opens

Expanding into the opulent light pervading everything,
Exploring, undulating, radiating
Floors, studios, corpses of fish,

The minutest detail of my life
As when a child I put
A flea in a fire to see if it would howl and burst.

Dissolving into infinity
Before the guardian Light Being
I am at the entrance of death.

Jumping into the wave but secretly
Holding on to myself, the vast Light
Erupts out of my eyes,

Extends into every verb, every idea of my mind. It is visceral,
A titan liberating antelope
And all the dark souls I feel

In a room at midnight, with my eyes closed,
Frightened and alone,
With a bad feeling about myself.

Jackals of ego and fear
Rise up after eating the new dead.
I have forgotten the rituals

Of the Pure Light, contract again,
Retaining but a few cells
Of my last birth and breath.

The date is unimportant
But I realize it came to a halt
On the shore, off the Atlantic,

With seagulls in squadrons circling,
Watching as the beachline exhaled nuns,
Children, the aging meatboxes of men.

The light comes back, the fin of a shark
Up from beneath the surface, then disappearing
Into the rudderless, unfathomable dark.

Out of the heart a jungle bird ascends,
A hundred colors, a thousand names,
Speaking in my own voice.

The man I remember no longer dreams of fire,
The man I remember is an orphan of hope and desire,
The man I remember feeds among the cactus, the petrified
        flowers.

The man I remember; a sea breeze suffused with scents of olive
        trees, fruit.
The man I remember; a pylon stretching out into open waters.

The man I remember; a sailor on acid seas, angry at the winds,
  the gales,

The scavenging gulls plucking the skull for sea worms and kelp
Lost in the eye sockets washed up on the beach.
The man I remember remembers

Thought-bones, mermen and teeth,
Tangled remains of lives,
Cinemas playing rooted in his own self.

A serpent-bird licks the inside top of my skull.
Blessed the blood releasing the memory,
Blessed the eye opening the flood.

Blessed the iguana remembered the forest,
Blessed the memory of flight through the acacia woods.
Blessed the onions, the kale, the iron pots over fires,

Blessed the academy of stars teaching us over the waters.
Blessed the villages, blessed the sea,
Blessed the siblings he sees

On the shores of a remote outpost
Below the star birth bardo in the body of Orion.
Windswept on the plateau

Rising beside the steady spine of the Nile,
By the limestone escarpment,
Among the sands, scorpions, the black cobras

With fanning skin behind their skulls,
The temple complex arose, stone
Cut in exact measurement. Rose quartz,

Obsidian, steles of granite, painted columns

Reaching to the imperishable stars.
Walking the forest of pillars,

Through a phalanx of gardens,
Amid scholars, elders, perfumes and camels
I eat honey cakes from strange, indigenous bees,

Study star maps on the temple walls.
I left my village the 12th season of Hathor
When the water inundation welled up.

My mother cried, my father swelled with hope.
My sister gave up braids of her hair
In the acacia woods, burned the resin of amber

With lotus root and kelp.
My Djedi master had seen me flying, flying in a dream,
Over rooftops, papyrus stalks, hippos

And sacred cows, ducks, barges
Coming down from Nubia and the upper cataracts
Over rock-strewn dangerous aberrations of the Nile.

From a reed boat he came to me
In white linen robe with a gold collar
Around his throat. On a scroll with bird figures,

Snakes, lines with quadrants in graced sequences
Unfolded on a table in the middle room
Of his vestibule Per Ankh by the river of blue and white I see

The Gizeh plateau, soul star place,
Benben/Omphalos navel of the world, reflected black waters
Behind the Milky Way, Duat etched in sand

With human bones stretching the timework

Of stars, hidden constellations
Still unborn in the swirling matrix of dark matter.

In the heart of Orion the seed of stars
Is collapsing, perplexed, reborn in the seething
Stomach and left shoulder of the sweet companion star Bellatrix.

In the secret dark place of Tehuti I rest
As my inner eye grows immeasurably bright.
I am lifted up, up through the channel,

The chamber of the sacred room
Near the king's place, granite and cedar wood
Structured into the space for a body within a body

Within a tomb. I am lifted up to black waters,
Into the scintillating current across the sky,
Companion in the boat of Re,

Translations enduring millions of years.
Suddenly I remember the crevice, the inner thigh of a temple girl
        I admired,
Then fall like a shooting star

Back to earth. Down through the firmament,
To basil and baskets, raisins and nails,
To enclosed gravitational places,

To wombs of women in labor,
To rice, to farms, to bits of flint,
The crusting scar tissue around my navel.

Forgetting… forgetting, fading and lost,
The tiny disturbances after a butterfly,
The scent of almonds on a summer day,

Pumice stone in a shower, a piece of bread,
A tincture of jasmine in a bowl of oil,
Grass waving in fields, small blue stones, iodine, salt,

Small of things on the cliff of sleep,
Smooth fingernails of the just turned dead.
I fall into the envelope

Of a captured Nubian prince's body. Down through the aperture
        of the skull
Before the bone plates close over
I fold, dwell for months in a saline sac

Until the ninth month bursting out under moonlight
Into the lung's first breath.
Amnesia has eaten my memory of other deaths.

Between camels, dark eyes, bags filled with myrrh
A caravan I am born into moves
Through the interior of a damaged, ancient dark city.

Slave-prince child born with an odd mark on his skull.

The city fathers marvel, the merchants compete.
I am sold to a star watcher
For twenty gold earrings, some potatoes, ginger root.

I learn accounting well, water the herds,
Attend to sheep. On my 12th inundation ride
Through the earth-bound mirror of the celestial arc

I am taught the hidden alphabet of books,
Stars, the femoral calculations living
In the rhythms at the base of temple columns, the mysteries.

When the stars pulse in my heart

And my age of bone and teeth agree,
I cross the east sea to Dravidian lands

Where the liquid snake in the spine freely moves.
The markets are full. Japatis, Dahl,
Saffron in cakes and peppermint oil,

Rubies, jades, carved tusks of beasts alongside
The indescribably poor, garlic, tomatoes,
Eggplants with white stripes down the center,

Porphyry and peanuts, scarves and ink.
Then the same girl again appears
Like some distant kin from beyond the star mountains.

I know her skin, her noises, her vowels
Returning to me like the languages rivers make,
Like dark echoes

In a bat-filled cave. I watch
Her hands move, temple bells crowd
My ears. Her eyes release a dark wine

And I am drunk by the sea
Filled with wreckage and cannot escape.
I marry her, she dies

Six years later in a fire; my heart
Is infested with carnivorous birds,
Wires, infected nettles, taxonomies of excess,

Broken tibias and ticks. Wrapped
In a memory of knives and silk
I set out on the caravans again. Six months of guilt

And travel, I come to a high pass

In the Hindu-Kush mountains. Our camels complain
With spit, nasal whines. The guides are restless,

Tired, near panic. In the brutal wind
Before the first snow I surrender my rage
Into a caucus of flowers, fire and smoke

Trailing upward like intestinal curves,
Dissipating, a black finger
Pointing into the night.

I hunt the wild extraction that will remove my fear.
Books, prayers, cemetery wanderings unclothed,
Exposed to the ghosts of foreign souls

Only take me so far. In Spring I travel south
To the knats of Bhrat along river banks blazing with funeral fires.
Children and aunts reduced to ash,

Bathers washing their hair in the effuse. Strings of carnations
Around my neck, the smell of scented flesh, honey,
Ghee. A green statue

Representing an invisible girl
Ignites, captures the flame of my attention
Then disappears into the natural world.

Birds see colors, fish smell under water,
False peregrinations of my mind inhabit my ear,
Burrow into catacombs

Beneath my imagination; darkness stranger than darkness.
Into the black estuary like an eel
Opening its mouth to the ocean

I swallow and am swallowed

By the Fundamental Clear Light surrounding my toes,
Evaporating saline in my eyes, my blood.

I go farther than the longing of shadows
For substance and order. Steer into the abyss
Without weapons or clothes. Then the memory of the omphalos,

The dark rites outside of Delphi
Beginning at Abydos rush my brain. The pit of serpents,
The rare birds, the onyx rings, the bones.

Orphaned by the body, abandoned patient in the asylum of
     mind,
I release my cup of consciousness
Into the infinite lifeblood of the sea; O Olokun

I am a stray particle lost
In the vast chamber of an ancient heart.
Then the battle of the plasma sea.

The shoreline of strange green rising waters.
Serpent-men pull me out of a trance.
Oval stones full of light

Ride above their eyes in the middle of their heads. Changing
     colors;
Their voices vibrate through me
Like lamentations in a winter famine.

The sea is rising, they are at war, know death.
Called back like migrating herds across the savannas,
Called back, lost voices of children echoed through the
     mountains,

Called back like an electron by hidden forces
Into the soul of the atom, I am called back

To the ancient world submerging into the sea.

Carrying the electricity of all the mothers
Who have ever evolved
I couple myself to fables found in darkened windows,

Pull back, astonished and grieving, from the pyramid
I once walked through, memorized
Like an iris memorizing primary colors.

Deeper laws merely touch the outer human.
Like frozen rain, like alabaster they worship
A different master, a different collector

Of razors, ambitions, souls that
Fill the harbors with musical instruments
Orchestrating the mating of bees and deer.

I fly back, an emerald in the purse of a thief.
I reappear, a returning life at the midnight of Civilization One.
The moon holds in the sky a distant sound, a wounded calf.

Priests and dragon-men, Nagas, magicians
Crowd into ships of silver and light,
Warp space around the rim, then rise

On a trail of celestial exhaust
Leaving rainbows, sheets of ions and cobalt, waves of beryllium,
The moody premonition of inexpressible loss.

I am back, back again. Light-work washed out in eternity,
Bent into forms through the curve of hours.
I return prodigal, adamantine,

Witness to genesis in a spasm of splendor.

III. *Above the Head of the Living & the Dead*

to my Ori

Outside my window crows gather,
Heads cocked upward, then higher,
Toward the light *Coming Forth by Day*,

Seen, then unseen wings against the dark.
The sun, a red lotus ponding in the sky.
I walk unknown remembering

Both the living and the dead, traveling
Along footpaths in black gardens
With huge insects, bipolar amphibians swimming

In water. The nameless unborn prepare here,
Dream until the orbit of hours
Funnels them down to cartilage, breastbone,

Cilia and aorta.
Without masks from the African embarkations,
Without the benediction of scorpions and bats,

Without the sound of wolves, the echo of canyons,
Without the spider's intuition of ropes and silk,
I feel the mineral language

Of the earth, her heroes climbing
The spine, spreading light, moving farther up
Into the enfolded spaces above the head

Where rivers of consciousness meet.
Depth, width and height
A crooked bank holding the mortgage

On lives until the debt is paid at death.
Sometimes we can escape into our own eyes

When staring into the mirror and a hand

Reaches out, grabs the heartbeat from
Our throats. The dead, the living
Walk back and forth through each other

Unaware of time, the century or even the shadows
Cast between lives in complex equations
Played out in casual day life.

Above time *time* doesn't move in straight lines,
Space isn't fused with depth, width and height.
Whispering just beyond the inner sanctum of the ear

Immortality is part of natural law,
An objective state,
Outside the flesh we come wrapped in.

Like succulent music,
Like the broken shell of oysters, fish,
In a tube of light spinning from the center of the earth it comes

Running through the spine into the neural curves above it,
A green river of fish, celestial birds,
Inhabitants of life in curled-up dimensions

Live through you, me, all of us. I am only dimly aware,
Keep my template, my hours,
My delusions and misjudgments.

They scour, purify themselves in solar fires,
Become a new testament for beings
Struggling up from the oceans and mud,

Warming continents, the early revelations
Of dark religions

In the grammar of magic and science.

I hear-tell in the brain's folds, nerve-work and the spaces above it
Oceans of currents spool in a database
For stars in flowing constellations

Where light-beings dwell in nine dimensions
Deeper than we feel in the human orders. Squeezing themselves
    down,
They commune with us through a bottomless

Chalice of radiance and bliss. Bloodcells of centurions
Long dead, a pinched-off fingernail of Christ,
A horse's knee, a congress of sparrows,

The subtle, eloquent breath of orchids and otters,
Hold our syntax and structure,
Narrowed, localized, collapsed into matter,

Allowing us to see for ourselves the bone work,
Sweat, the animal muscle in our hands, our toes,
The cold noise leaking from our skulls.

Prophecies adhere in DNA.
Financial markets with maps explain for a fee
The geography of poverty, the alchemy between

Logic, welfare and labile gold. An empty bell,
Trains lined with caskets moving through the night
Are all signposts out of hell.

Strange waters are above the head,
Waters with angry children, thorns growing,
Waters with luminous fish attracted to the moon.

IV. *Ten Songs to the Stones*

i. *To The Gatekeeper*

Master of the fish and the angels, hear me,
Messenger of the dark equations, witness my word.
Sprinter among the clouds,
Seducer of the Magi,
Sorcerer secluded in every eyelash and occasion,
Whisper and open me.
Explore the cave of my heart like an incandescent bird,
Wings full of fire, instinct and hope.
Bring me the perfume, the laughter
In the labyrinth between hyacinths and water.
O bodiless inventor in the nine dimensions,
Gatekeeper of the nine gateways of the body,
Inhabit me with an alien beauty, eat my soul.

ii. *Transformation of the Black Pearl*

Black pearl, self-luminous and alone,
Moving beyond names and derivations
In a language of resonances,
Replace solid things with axons and nouns.
In an apothecary of spirit with naked herbs,
Resins, sounds rounded and emptied out,
Mix and weave them in a cure for wild geese
Flying above the autumn sunset,
Suddenly confused in the carnage of colors.
Bring the new cold sweeping in from the north.
Lock it into the ice machine of winter
With its rounded waters holding on to the trees
In the tiny hard white fruit of the rain.

iii. *A Woman is Walking*

A woman is walking with almond eyes, the musical ambition of
    the sea.
A woman with broken accents and a basket full of tomatoes
Is declaring her innocence among strangers
In a marketplace of thieves.
A woman is imitating a spider endlessly weaving
A shimmering basket of talismans, starfish,
Operas of the faithful in a Capella singing.
A woman is bathing in the ocean, small fish
Swim up to her, try to enter her watery vagina,
Inveigle themselves into cities of mermen,
Dolphins, hidden travelers crossing the solar expanse.
A woman is testifying at midnight before the trees,
Clear moon applauding her with shadows,
Warnings between the branches, the fallen leaves.

iv. *A Woman is Walking*

A woman is walking through her own organs,
Hearing gods speak in blood, flows of the liver,
Intestinal pulsations, endocrine harmonies in the lymph nodes,
Armpits, breasts and mouth. There is a sacred river
In her thighs, a fountain in her heart.
Her secret name echoes in the space behind her eyes.
Her tongue is spun out of a codex of names
Unheard of since the death of the last tsar.
A woman is kneeling, entering the mineral language of the first
    dimension,
Speaking to diamonds, salt, the pure will of carbon,
The legends of the elements burst out after the star of creation.
A woman is praying to her ancestors on a hilltop,
Overlooking a graveyard, a garden, a pond
Where the recently dead gather, released in the fullness of
    autumn.

v. *A Woman is Walking*

A woman is walking out of her own skin,
Changing it from copper to bronze, alabaster to ebony,
Fulfilling the prophecies of the pharaohs and philistines,
Calling to her sisters in odd and beautiful harmonics,
Strange sounds brought back from the afterlife.
A woman is adjusting her undergarments
Before a deep blue mirror. Men
From future generations, aroused, come forth
From the sea, from the underside of the mirror,
Wrap her bones in delicate embraces, murmur
Quiet benedictions from a tribe of unknown poets.
A woman is moving, pilgrim among elements and enemies,
Jewel in the wreckage, oracle in the garbage,
Undercurrent of rivers murderous with bliss.

vi. *Meditation*

In the savannah of the body are rivers,
Blue veiny rivers, rivers overflowing with arms
Reaching out to the animal powers.
There are herds of great beasts, constellations of migrating birds,
Primates on the edge of the forest, violent, intolerant of man.
There are gorges flecked with bones and flint, Homo Sapiens
        markings.
There are arrowheads, copper tools,
Ruins of men under grass and stone that tracked the orbit of the
        stars
While sitting on dried antelope skin. In the stairway of night
They put one foot atop the other,
Applied the undulating sequence of internal locks, anus, stomach
        and chin,
Held the breath in, then out and milked the tongue,
While the eyes, like lovers, fused above the head.
A vermilion apogee of flesh awoke, uncoiled from within them
        the luminous Living One.

vii. *Meditation*

Sacrifice your attention to me.
Come weightless and ecstatic
Into the dark canals of my city.
Surrender your thoughts like noble children
Into quiet parks, ponds where they wash themselves
Into oblivion, emerge reborn into saints and scholars
Writing in a language that keeps changing form.
Release your interior into my presence,
Exhale your bones and sensations. Ride the last wave of intuition
Into a cauldron of pure witness and fire
Extending into every permutation of infinity.
Winter. Solitude. Everything arising at once;
Scaffold of atoms, Black horsemen in a field,
Yellow leaves on oak trees caught shivering against the sky.

viii. *Monday Evening*

A suicide in the moonlight
Walks toward the trees, beneath him blue stones shiver.
A light goes out in a farmer's house.
A black cow stares into the eyes of a fallen crow
Decaying in the leaves. The hay rustles.
A virgin bleeds at the thought of diamonds.
The entrails of a rodent stain the barn floor.
A hawk digests. A rabbit, hidden under a barrow,
Prays for tomorrow as the sun wallows
On the other side of the world.
A priest undresses in a hospital room,
Slips into the breath of a dying nun.
The wind swings a body like swollen fruit
On the lowest branches. A lost child in the wilderness coughs.

ix. *The Dark Religions Flying*

There is a doctrine in the wind. I have felt it flying.
I have felt it with my hands reaching out

To other fingers and the small blue beings
Invisible to my eye carrying in themselves
The amethyst of honesty and truth. I have lost
On frequent mornings this inward balance,
Forgotten the angels, accepted the truce between
Vampire and allegory, nails and honey,
Passed forward and up into the bag of veins and nostrils
In the shrinking cage of my body.
With the deeper dream dissolving, surrendered,
I wake into the propaganda of radios and time,
Delusions of watches and money.
I have failed the dark religions flying, flying.

x.   *Song Before Sleep*

Master of my lineage, author of my voyage
Through the hearts of women in whom I discovered myself, lost
        and loved;
Secret teacher of the spaces above the head and beyond,
Dissolve me at the top of my skull. Erase the line
Between the luminous Ones and the dense forest of my organs
        and cells.
Protect me in my travels, bathe my interiors,
Warm and nurture my path among bones and shells
Left by the dead still walking, dreaming of former lives.
Lead me into the bright lake beyond human desire
Where there is only light, intuition and beauty.
Bless my former bodies, all their adventures
In the flesh, the blood of my strong invisible hours.
Welcome me into the house of only mirrors, insight,
Ascended mind. Bleach me of terrors; teach me to abandon all I
        resist.

V.   *Remember Me*

For Alyse

i

Remember me as a mirror, dark and full of rivers,
Lost rivers, rivers guarded by birds
And spirits moving nightly
Through solemn, vestigial lands.
Remember me as ocean, as whisky, as the wave of dark honey
Bees make out of sacred clover
Wishing to incur favor
From solitary, distant gods.
Remember me as cloth stolen
From vanquished warriors in the wars
Over beauty, the genius of stones.
Make my sorrow a language of bells.
Construe my appetite as a sign of returning thunder.
Invite my wonder, my graying hair, my fear of tomorrow
Into the bright vestibule of your attention
And I will carry your memory with me
As a child carries his mother's scent
Through wars, famines, cold orphanages.
Remember me as a starfish remembers
Its original form, as a handful of coal
Remembers its birth among ferns, giant lizards, great beasts.
Remember me as a dream once dreamt by the Buddha
From which he drew the water of serene detachment,
Then washed through it, without struggle, passing out of the
        stream of matter.
Let me be a flute in the quiet orchestra of your eyes.
Bequest rain and small insecurities to me.
Pull me into the harbor beyond day and night
And I will pull you even more gently to me

As an intimate gravity pulls the constellations
Across the sky toward the Great Attractor.
Inherit me as the sea inherits
Gulls in their slow decent
Into whitecaps hunting fish,
Crustaceans, bits of men and fragments on the reefs
Tossed overboard in some forgotten, arbitrary war.
Remember me as a stroke victim remembers sounds
Passing endlessly inward towards his own name
And nothing more.
Remember me in soapstone, discarded bicycle wheels,
Blue plastic cups that have begun to peel.
Remember me as the rain passes overhead
And I will hold you
As my first memory of fire and jasmine brought together.

VI. *Remember Me*

ii

Remember me as the body,
As the dying lion and the new gazelle
Brought face to face with the thorn of extinction
Racing across the plane of existence
Between trees, high grasses, ponds of mud
Where the crocodile infests amid flowers of unspeakable splendor.
Remember me as the body
Thickening, then grown lean with medical incantations,
Aprils of the heart,
Recurring summers of sexual vegetation,
Anatomies and nervework,
Neural reinventions, somatic autobiographies,
The literature of profane livers, intestines,
Fingernails and bile salts
Navigating through the world, rediscovering
Swans and villages, children and apples,
Seeing in the cells, the bloodwork, the elastic veins
And wrinkles and watches living in the eyes,
The dark inheritance that is always Spring.
I am the new wine, the dense tomato,
The uterus of porous and vernal speech.
Remember me as the body
With hard places like agate and feldspar.
Remember me in units of granite and chrome, clumsy lodestone,
Magnetic attractions so clear and vital
The moon bends down on certain nights
To see what draws it irresponsibly to earth.
Remember me as the body
Lover's touch after twenty years of separation,
Locked in prisons, held behind moats,
Pent up acids and kisses,

Tied in ropes the color of cinnamon and sweat,
Dried out, evaporated, steadied in violence
Like a spear of steel.
Remember my body as a dark gospel
Full of animal seeds in a coil of flesh,
Permeable and superstitious with organs
Suggestive of hickory and licorice,
Hair the texture of wool. Remember me as a harvest
Reaped under the watchful eye of a burning god.

VII. *Remember Me*

iii

Remember me as a vampire
Washed ashore on a moonless night,
Stars dissipating, the wind soundless, cruel,
The deer urinating out of fear, then heading south.
Walking, as a spider among the unquiet dead,
Longing for disciples,
Longing to return to the rivers of the living,
Correcting the stutter brought to the heart,
I move, a dark liquid between shadows, by stitches and timber,
By an opened blue vein,
By the cataract of the will I have held by the neck
When voices move through me
Like an Aryan wind over the winter steppes.
There is a dark link in my appetites
For the blue and tubular,
For the wet and sexual in the blood
Holding the strength of many lives,
For the scent of basil and garlic in the teeth,
For the hollow eyes of Azazel and the blind.
Damp troops under the earth
Rise, become mists and shadows,
Twisting under doors, entering rooms of those drifting into sleep,
The feral corpse
New to the tomb and spiritually unwed.
Hold my hands, feel my face melt away.
Feel ice in my tailbone, the wolf in my ear,
The bottom feeder with snout cruising above the waterline.
The sun pulls up on the horizon.
I move, a swollen thing,
Dragging in its belly stones, souls, bits of memory
From brains, alabaster fingernails,

Broken plastic from old phones, molting bones,
Slender nettles of copper wire.
Stand back.
Watch me, carefully, like a knowing crow.
Examine my body like a disinterred pope.
Distrust every lyrical assessment by me
Until we see each other naked,
Exquisitely wet,
Fall backwards in slow motion through the mirror.

VIII. *Meditations on Genesis*

Nothing can be born of nothing and so
I was reborn from the world beyond essence and light.
From beyond splendor and revelation I came,
Riding a pure spasm of darkness and imagination,
Carrying in me the fist of creation out of the sleep of a watery
    serpent
Coiled and floating on an ocean of oblivion
Before contractions giving birth to the world.

Crocodile in the heart, remorseless, androgynous
With bodies pulsating in the abyss, I split and took solidity
In seven shaping gods streaking through the firmament
Bringing forms and new religions to the seas, the rocks,
Guttural sounds rolling in the throat, primeval conjunctions,
The web of matter within matter
Running through the river of stars.

Sex and death, tools of impregnation and progression
Rushed out in a singular fingerprint
Marking entrance into this tiny fragment,
This rind and ash,
This tissue thrown out in the speech of the void.
Beast, Yakut, harlot of fire,
Seven-headed and winged with scales of flame and flower,

Scarlet and black, a furnace of souls,
Wild conflagration of expansion and awe,
A bird in snake form with undulating curls,
Flashes of energy, whirlpools and spirals,
Matter emerging out of my breath in vibrating *AUMs*.
Stripped of electrons and fragrances before the tooth of death,
The soul behind minerals was all darkness and depth.

Time, a sheer being of duration and force.

Then seven blue stars in a cluster formation
All dreaming in motion and the same direction,
Took possession of a local cube of heaven with spiral arms,
Pushed hot fornication in bits of carbon, molecular gas,
Seeds of shapes, nanodiamonds, the swoosh of equations.
Pure field contracted, knots arose, then roots and location.

Glass became mirrors, darkness invented shadows,
Cellars of the future dead filled with blind widows and sailors.
Down the seven sisters bathing came, wading
Into the spinning net of the spider, the black cathedral,
With the opulent expediency of an owl swooping
In a dark glide for the secretive rodent, the azure fish,
The hungers of silver for the light after polish and stone.

And into this came death feeding
On the anthracite echo of life-force extracted,
Tossed about across emerald waters,
Bruised, ripped out and intoxicated, then bashed
Against the stone wreckage of genesis in the morning.
Out of a crimson stream in the aurora borealis,
Magnetic and northward-leaning, spreading like lava,

I came into the earth where the equinoxes circle out.
Long and elliptical along the axis I came descending into the
        belly of the world
Roiling with the stolen fire of the stars,
Spinning about the vortex twisting matter and gravity
Into a spiraling helix, conch shells,
Serpents coiling around the calyx and cartilage of the spine.
Folds and funnels in time connect ancient spirits, arid lands,

To the glass and manganese of modern times.
Criss-crossing the earth's skin with lines of force,

Whirlpools arose, opened out in 1746 pores.
Dragon lairs, eyes of pearls, caves of granite
In the deep red mountains over streams feed by glacial ice
Running in veins, black crevices underneath the earth,
Carrying the hidden vibration of all names.

In the black cock of evolution
Spirit rode upward into shapes from the moisture
And maelstrom of hot stones, geysers,
Pressures of water breaking like bones, pepper on the tongue,
Sweet basil and larva,
The first lavender of consciousness to rise up from the dust.
Into the body, like a ferret into the pathways of the underworld,

The hot snake of one eye
Ran and reawakened
In the dark inner vine inhabiting the backbone,
The musical mirror of the living waters
Carrying the current of the stars out of creation,
Then back to its source in the cycle of womb,
Death, radiance and transformation.

Seven coils around the river of life,
Seven organs and seven sounds, seven seas flesh the earth,
Seven planes of light open above the body.
The tongue becomes the eye,
Wild Buddhas invade the land.
There is a brilliant confession in the autumn sky
That all this will die and rise again.

IX. *Poetry is a Kind of Wine*

Poetry is a kind of wine,
A blue redemption, an irresponsible form of religion
Teaching trees, as well as men
And dogs and the winds that scream
At shadows over the deserts,
That it comes
Carrying a message of eternity and sacrifice.
Like a woman standing over a woman,
Like a dark animal with the future of beauty in its stomach,
Poetry came to me, moist,
Incandescent, an original bird,
Startling and resplendent, with foliage and plumage
Surrounding its nest, a great orange of feathers
Multiplying, sending out waves of itself
Beyond the bleachers,
Beyond the rest homes,
Flailing in the distance like a foghorn
Fallen unconsciously into sleep.
Years passed.
Then it came back, back to me,
Calling to me, to my name, to the beating
In my thorax, the plum in my navel,
The viscera and vortex in the plunge of my belly
Demanding to speak to me in my first tongue.
"I am the music your father resisted
When death came to him,
A sudden strumpet demanding her money back,
Taking his heartbeat for coinage down
A narrowing alley of existence and circumstance
Until it reached the blueprint, the
Disturbing punctuation days and hours make
On their curious voyage to god."

Then, then
Through the rupture between time
And the decisions we make,
The discarded shirt of an orphan came to me,
Covered with numerals, alphabets, poorly conceived stitches,
And the relic or insignia of a vanished prophet.
With buttons sharper than a cat's eye
Its compass drilled into the pulse
In my throat.
It told me poetry is the compact language of the higher gods,
Pushed down, riven like a fever dream,
Into the stone, the chiseled flesh of the moment.
It has neighborhoods, ethics, faces, dimensions,
Astounding fruits and the memories of tribes
No longer circling the miracle of the oceans.
A tablet, obsidian and basalt, deep as a river,
Moves out of the night sky toward the bolt
Keeping lock over my heart and the ordinary stars.
I have not done or loved nearly enough.
I can no more explain myself
Than justify the color blue,
Or feel why a pomegranate has more seeds than an apple,
Or why fish prefer the sea
Over the oceans of galactic space,
Or why I was born under a particular moon,
Why black flowers undress us after we have entered the grave.
But this I do know
That when we are burnt ash to ash,
And we walk as our ancestors walked
Over the same grove of bones,
And the centuries have grazed above us
In herds of new inventions and innumerable clocks,

That the grape skin around us has given up
A new wine and we travel on seas
With no name in our language.

X. *Forms of a Woman*

For Alyse

Finding your name among the habits of strangers,
In odd and ancient books,
In the blood of vipers submerging under waters,
In the circles and calibrations of spiders,
I have not been afraid.
I have followed you,
Watched you in moonlight
Drifting through the ruins of a temple.
Your hands make black flowers surrender,
Their voices disturbed by an illegal form of beauty.
When I touch your arm my fingers gather honors
Reserved for soldiers returning home to die
On the altars of their fathers.
In empty chairs after worship
I sense your gaping absence.
In the presence of scorpions
I feel your disarming voice.
I don't know why candlelight reminds me of your body,
Except that its flame is constantly changing,
Its message older than man.
There are a thousand different interpretations
In the flutter of your eyelash, endless weapons
In a casual glance. I have made a study
Of the rivers you leave behind
When you walk up the stairway brushing aside the air,
Or walk in a dream, nude with tangled hair,
Through some autumnal garden.
Your shoulders are a landscape,
Your arms the embrace of willows,
Your face a sacred coastline sketched
By an artist of immortal technique.

Your hands play at secrets
When you motion towards me. Your lower back,
A sweet river of deliverance and sweat.
I am constantly amazed
Your eyes do not swallow whole armies;
Your breasts are prayers
Birds and religions make.
There are mercies in your fingerprints,
Strange showers even in your breath.
Children and their terrors find asylum in your heartbeat.
There is an immaculate form of marble
When you are angry and stare. Red
Is the color of your sorrow, keeping me
Off balance, guessing at your next request.
And at death,
At death you pass back into an interior life
Knowing ancient waters, funerals of warrior kings.
You take the future there with you, discuss it
With beings living in light, outside of time.
Your velocity is hope, your thighs warm shadows.
White electricity inhabits your mind.

XI. *The Gospel of the Dark Orisha*

i. *The Broken-In Vault*

There is an asylum of serpents
Inside my skull. Legend holds
After midnight, in the wake of nuns singing
Low and off key, a flood of bats will arrive,
Infest the sky with eyeless blackness,
Then a prophet will appear rambling on
About minor deities, the strategies of hope.
I exhume my consciousness
From the graves of children,
Wash my fingers in a weak acid of desire,
Dry them in the afterglow of a burn- out intelligence.
Lifting up my arms
To the river dragging the world into the morning
I realize there is a war going on.
Broken bones lay scattered
Among the ashes of books,
Wings with torn feathers collect behind stones.
Something has dropped here,
Exploded out, reminiscent of the innards of a clock.
Then I realize the whole scene
Is a T.V. episode
Ricocheted off a distant planet.
Evolution and religion have gone into business together,
Issued common stock, taken bids
On the most promising hedge fund products.
It seems they've won.
Reptiles, after Ages of longing,
Have ascended into birds in a spiral of lightness,
Realizing their ancient dream to fly.
Mammals have booked passage
With their baggage of hair and souls

On journeys that will take them lifetimes to complete.
Fish assume positions far beyond their normal reach.
I am confounded by all this, and the owls,
And the wisdom of carnivores.
I sense Buddhas under the fingernails of primates
Having yet to learn
The awkward magic of speech.
Something is growing in every mollusk, a pearl,
Or something broken and sharp, howling for birth,
Needing no armor, organs or teeth.
A secret peels away from the frontal lobes,
The buttocks, the massive feet,
Finding an outlet in the dark tongue
A fallen mercenary has inherited
In the cruel, offbeat wetlands of his sleep.

ii. *Spiritual Practice*

For the Ori who has no name

Forgive my kneecaps, the weird knowledge of my shoulders,
The awkward calculus of my ribcage,
My breathing.
The body has discovered
Another form of logic.
When I bring my toes together
Under the muscular cathedral of organs
Near the pelvis, the hipbones; after we agree
About the stretches, the blood vessels, the glands,
And agreeing to all this,
I tighten my lower backbone,
Relax the breath, then
Close and fix my eyes above my forehead

As if it was the sea.
A subtle white river swims up from my coccyx
Without hands or money,
Full of fables, birds sounds,
Images with vague, floating reptilian scenery.
It becomes thin, luminous, a flute
Full of villages and tongues. Then
My mid-back oscillates
From side to side,
Magpies caught in a bag,
Ambivalent about the earth, trying to escape.
Then a nightingale hops up to a higher branch,
Catches me formulating music,
Foreign vocabularies in my throat.
In time an oyster collapses, spits out its gut,
Sends its pearl drilling upward
Into the narrow space where the angels shipwreck
In their descent, emptying out,
Religions feeding on the debris.
A yellow bird with a black wing
Meets me on a continent
Without mornings, the sun full of bells
From coast to coast.
Then the vowels, the bellows, the gutturals
From beyond the deserts arrive,
Dissolve the brain cells, the blood locks.
Even the echo of me.

iii.   *The Book of Laws*

The moment the addiction subsided
Warm brown women flowed out of his ear
And settled into the pond behind the house.

Jasmine was in the air, and lilac,
And torches from night weddings.
A corpse of roses lay at his feet.
Fingering through the rubble,
The broken cups, the used tea bags
On the library floor that had been moved outside
When the tornado came through,
He found the book of laws his grandfather
Had hidden many years ago
Until a stroke bombed through
His parietal lobe just above the temporal area gateway
Above the left ear, the place
Where his tunnels opened out to the wider world.
He noted the coincidence
Of their medical dramas,
Wondered if both would have gravestones
Facing the yellow mountains
With their backs turned to the sea.
The last Saturday in autumn
When the leaves achieved parity
With the other deaths walking before them
A shadow would come out from an interior dimension
That could not be re-hydrated
Or surrounded in any language or kind of name.
The book of laws came from here.
Here it could be squeezed, punctuated,
Quoted correctly from the voice of God.
He looked at the pages.
Letters moved around.
He grabbed the bindings, the edges,
Holes and warn out spots appeared.
He turned it upside down, shook it gently,

Rain fell out, made watermarks appear.
He lifted it to his nose,
One nostril went into spasm,
Slapped strange circumstances across his brain.
Finally he understood. His navel hurt him,
His throat could not clear.
He noticed three of his knucklebones were broken and bleeding.

iv. *Nephilim* *

I open my hand
And it flies into me, into my skin,
My eyes, the corners of my mouth,
Becomes wings and bats, desperate situations,
Left-over excuses for failure, greed,
The thin blue glass of loss.
Nephilim, apostle of smoke and iron,
Broken avenger with hammer and thorns,
Curled feet, eyes without pupils,
Nightmare of scorpions scraping the sky
At the onset of death.

       ***

I open my head
And a black museum falls into me,
Down eternities, down hours, down milliseconds
Into an underground stable, its horses
Stolen from the last pharaoh's dream of conquest
Over deserts with nomads, lakeshores
Filling with naked girls captured and willing.

       ***

---

*   In ancient times it was known or believed that a race of giants or fallen gods had once mated with human females spawning the Nephilim. Twice they are mentioned in the bible and appear repeatedly in Jewish and Christian writings as well as popular films and the symptoms of psychiatric patients.

I open my throat,
A waterfall of leeches and mushrooms,
Hallucinogenic animals I have never seen,
Take up residence, inspect my bones,
Make my uvula, my larynx, my voice box,
Their center and hive,
Send out bees, drones,
In evil armies and harmonics.
Nephilim, torn between the twin gods,
Dark energy, dark matter,
Bleeding from organs punctured by light,
You come dressed and wet, a raven
Full of shadows, full of nails, full of orphans and offal
Trailing inscrutable noises we hear
Upon leaving a bad dream.
Nephilim fallen to earth through a scar
On the underbelly of night,
Eating obituaries, remembering Goliaths,
Shaking off talismans and rings,
Failed religions, molecules of flesh,
The singeing tongues of brutal things.
Free and naked, unafraid of wind and rain,
Copulating in ravines, in caves, in sacred places
Of obsidian and smooth stone you sing
With statues all around you
In the natural world. Among the waters,
On meadows with hyacinths,
In forests without names,
In rivers the color of dark berries and oils
You huddle, navigate in the breath of strangers,
Exchange heat; watch it rise in the air,
A lurid smoke, an opulent prayer,

Dense with beauty like a bible
Devoid of violence or sin.

***

Nephilim, Nephilim,
Loosened from penitentiaries
Full of funereal birds, dark eels, other abominations
Priests exorcise or keep hidden
In vestibules out of sight, out of wavelength,
Out of reach from all but the archangels
Frozen in brass and stone atop wooden sepulchers
Left over, stolen from churches burned
Back into the earth during the dark ages.
Rabid angel with red wings
Come forth, a healing fire, a white poison,
A gamble of divinity
In the coiling worm of the summer earth.

***

Nephilim, muscular heart of salt
And small, dark indentations
Pulling like gravity
Toward the cruel Galilean under the skin.
Micromanager of stillbirths, calculating Anubis,
Interbreed of slave women and cocks
Plunging in from another dimension,
I have gone out with you on winter nights,
Amid ice and razors,
Past cameras, crows, geometrical stones
Carved into the side of roads, past ditches,
Sewer pipes, necromancers unaware they are sleepwalking in a
    dream.
I have gone flying with you under the dark oceans,

Under waves, under currents, under urges
Reaching back before the Pliocene age
Where the needlefish watch us, oarfish invade our eyes,
Galleons of the unborn hover and wait.
Then, then when the microbes and angels
Have been bleached of mercy,
The delusions of permanence dissolved
Like a gong in the wind,
I open my soul
And I see Nephilim, I see the vast uncut ribbon
Of being and thirst
Flowing in a stairwell
From the navel of the earth through the kidneys of babies,
Mythical cows, gallows of innocent and condemned men,
Shepherd's wandering since the beginning time,
Women worshipping minerals, obelisks under sand,
Dinner plates, ghettoes, fornicating sergeants,
Spiritual wine and that strange yellow blood
Coming out of lovers who suicide by the sea,
By the waves, near the rocks,
Feeling the dark magnetism sweep them into immortality.

      ***

There,
There in the backdrop of horses and money,
Among masks and mosquitoes, textile plants,
Raw potatoes, among flowering bees, stamens and starlings,
Copper pots, spoons, ladles full of strawberries,
Iodine, oranges, sand in the stomach of oysters becoming pearls
    and babies,
Among monoliths, yeasts, electrical switches, acids and omens
And forgotten doctoral degrees,
You were born

Into the tribe of those red women who fuck out of appetite
And the moonlight beliefs
Forgotten by all but time and the rituals of menstruation
Carried out monthly on the edge of the sea,
Remembered in libraries of blood and iron, sacred to Abydos,
Original theology of the Tigress and Euphrates.

***

Nephilim come up from the earth, descend from the sky,
Pass with me in light through the thighs of women,
O messenger of electricity, skinless god,
Luminous infidel with the throat of a thief.

v. *A Fragment of Memory from the Night Walks of Valeria Messelina**

Anyone can visit the dead.
So when
The war between the cocks was over
The vanquished were carried,
One by one, outside and burned
In the sacred burial groves
By the sycamores, beyond the swamps.
The underground waters
Sucked down their souls, ferried them off
To distant springs where
Strong-boned women come to wash their long hair
In the dark streams
Coming up from the purified ore
With the scent of Orpheus

---

*   Valeria Messalina, born into the royal Julian bloodline, was the 3rd wife of the emperor Claudius when they married in AD 37 or 38, during the brutal reign of Caligula. Beautiful, powerful, promiscuous and apparently gifted in the erotic arts she intrigued to have her son Britannicus succeed Claudius on the throne. Accused of multiple sexual indiscretions in a series of scandals and a palace coup, she was eventually executed by centurions at the command of the emperor. Nero later succeeded to the throne.

Leaking from their skulls.
Waves upon waves across the open fields
Thriving like poppies
The cocks come rising in sails,
Straight and pulsating
Under the fangs of the moon.
Warrior's cocks, cocks of priests,
Cocks of angels roaming the heavens
Dreaming down into the thighs of women
Stretched out upon the earth,
Coiling into the watery vortex of the world.
On her night walks alone, outside of Rome,
Between rituals about omens,
Vaginas, hidden oils and skin,
A wicked adolescent schemes and roams,
Dreaming of the Caesars, the African cats,
Catching the new spirits before they reenter
The hot orbit of the blood and lung.

vi. *There is a Bird inside the Body*

There is a bird inside the body flying with us
From life to life to life.
There is a dark music
Filling the bones when we remember lost friends
We loved and fucked, our knees young,
Hair unscripted, thickening
In the air.
There is a perilous link discovered between
Humility and honor,
When the body no longer returns
From sexual rivers full of new fish
And semen gathered from stars

On our night walks through eternity.
Seeing a squirrel
I become envious of his freedom, his stupidity
When he hops from branch to branch,
Mindless of last week,
Mindless faith in tomorrow.
And then, and then sometimes I wonder in the morning
If I have awakened out of life,
Can look back on the bed and see
My sleeping form, half curled,
A fallen moon, motionless and warm,
As though I had just left it
To strangers to find, wrap up
In white linen, carry to some isolated spot
On the curve of an ancient river
And bury there deep enough so that each year
The waters rush over it but never
Conduct it all the way to the sea.
It is in moments like these
A bird flies through my body
Reminding me how each death I pass through
Is the edge of a high cliff
From which I see the whole valley of life,
Life deeper, fuller, more rounded and stretched out
Over eons than I could have remembered
In the eyes of friends lost to flesh,
Time, the shifting rock forms of my fate.
Religion is closer to me than avocados
Or plastic or the infinite uses of electricity
Keeping my computer and money
Organized in hierarchies of glass, Technicolor and concrete.
A wounded animal, mammalian and limbic,

Moves out of my lips
Towards vast unexplored continents
Where things, dark and ambivalent,
Wait to be discovered. Tracks in the forest,
Footprints on the beach, disturbed waves
On the coast say a magnificent beast
Has passed this way, near exhaustion,
Looking for a last welcoming place
To die. Yes to die again and again
Until the ritual finally recoils upon itself,
Light folding back into light,
Duty and destiny of the flesh
Working its will
Into the wider circumference of matter and consciousness.
A bird inside my body carries me
Past rain, past islands,
Past amphibians collecting near ponds
With black leaves fallen, decayed,
The life under them cold and unafraid
Of the winter coming.
There is a bird, holy and contemptuous,
Carrying me into the center of the earth,
Center so beautiful
I cannot resist becoming a thief.

vii. *The Journey of Adam into Exile; An Alternative Story*

1.

Driven from paradise furious, fuming
Through the tunnel of wings, the shrilling cicadas,
The black angels within him scratched,
Pulled at the scar of his navel.
He heard a blue language

In his heart, stitched a stolen bay leaf
In front of his crotch.
Adam, thrown out, stood up amid his losses and counted,
Looked for the living across
A battlefield of men, severed heads, dead horses.
The days of ivory and miracles were past.
The sun, a military star,
Boiled in its skin on the horizon.
Sycamore trees full of Spanish moss,
Alert with birds and small carnivores,
Hung above the water pool, the blue fountainhead of innocence
Now a swamp. The snake,
Full of apples and knowledge,
Was laughing, the darkness coming;
Eve lay curled up on a rock,
Hissing with resentment, cunning.
With divorce out of the question
And the wind picking up, speaking
Its oracles in broken tongues,
He leaned into the future with his one good arm,
Pulled himself into the morning.

2.

Then, and then
It rained, it was autumn,
It was nighttime, he was cold. He drove.
The headlights of his car scraped the black tongued road.
Like the silver intestine of a ghost
Caught in the x-ray screen of his window shield
A serpent arose, moved across the pavement,
Then buried itself in a tree stump
Near a swollen brook

Gushing with water and juices like an over-active gland.
He recognized him, a fallen angel, an errant friend
From the wars for paradise
In the supraluminous realms where there were no 'things,'
Every being moving faster than light.
He escaped from the car, followed him
Through wet grass and thorns,
Red berries and thicket,
Until he came to a granite outcrop
Smooth and slippery as burnished glass.
A tribe of vipers was here;
A copper river of scales undulated in leaves,
A green escapist coiled in the grass,
A king snake stretched out oozing on feldspar
Like a satrap in a great hall.
Archetypes and ancestors claimed the walls, the carpets,
Indolent, wise, with a curious appetite
For the underbelly of love.
Through the atmosphere damp with smoke and lavender
He listened, heard the legends of their fall to earth
In spasms of lightning
Flung from the void.
The Master of forms in the unscripted worlds
Had confused demons with the chaos of angels;
Every bird became its opposite,
Every thorn gave birth to an angry spider,
Then washed up on shore,
A liberating pearl. Their
Animal forms in muscular tubes, exquisite nerves,
Seized the reins of power.
Nothing could stop them. Not beauty, not victory,
Not the smell of garlic, the conviction of enemies,

Not even the voice of girls from the other side of the dark.

3.

Teaching the hidden science of vibration,
The secret behind the mummies' clothes,
The dialect of tree frogs, the blood in the cloisters,
The hummingbird's mastery of impossible flight,
The fallen masters, avatars in the mud,
Funneled all their muscle into a single seeing eye.
Beneath them dark sisters of every Age
Lived in the hive, the coil at the spinning vortex of the earth.
They called and crawled and came up
To watch his ascension
Like golden apostles streaming back to God.
Then unzipped from the bardos,
Liquid, sonorous as virgin wine,
They gathered together,
Burned their epitaphs of old skins and veins,
Took upon themselves new bodies of rose oil,
Ecstasy and light,
Mended the tissue of light torn from light.

4.

With this new knowledge, the spectacle over,
Birds left eternity to wither on earth
In marches, valleys, twisted tree trunks beside streams,
In bodies of excrement, lilies, recycled dirt,
Grew angry at the imbalance at the center of the world.
They demanded a new choir, a new jury,
A new form of justice,
Devoid of rubber, easy formulas and alloys of brass.
They demanded of Adam a new world

Where sin and beauty came together,
Where lovers are stalked
By the truths they have fled,
Where thin and leggy messages from the dead
Can cross oceans, dreams and political parties,
Reach your ear in oval kisses
Set alchemists singing, erase stigmata,
Leave ghosts and warriors howling on the shore.

5.

If I have forgotten your blood is an illusion,
The taste of the sea
In a glass of warm red wine,
Forgive me. If I am no longer Shephard of your dreams,
It is my loss. If I have loved you
Without balance or judgment,
Let it be a sacrifice for something greater
Than you can see or imagine.
If my breath is extinguished by the sea
In the presence of liars and priests
Offering talismans and prayers to the open waters,
Let my organs, my willpower surrender its landscape
Into the mystery of your flesh.
I will release all music into the silence
Gathering around you.
Forgive my palpitations, my injuries, the redness of my guilt.
See beyond my skull, its coarse reminders of blood.
See me clear and immaculate,
The desert after a rainstorm,
And I will come to you washed and forgiven,
Ready to accept the judgments of oystermen
And waves, ready to learn

From the journeywork of fish circling the oceans
In warm currents searching for food and sacraments.
Forgive the language of my body, its indecipherable vowels,
Seeking to explain
The radical gift of your presence.
Love me beyond all earthly knowledge
And I will reclaim an angel hidden within you.
Believe in me again,
A dark seed, a radiant Osiris,
And I will abandon every myth of finitude and death.

viii. *Obatala Singing of the Underworld*

> *"One luminary clock against the sky*
> *Proclaimed the time was neither wrong nor right.*
> *I have been one acquainted with the night."*
> Robert Frost, *Acquainted With the Night*

When the blood has forgotten all its secrets,
When the final ambitions of the body

Fade, one by one, sword by sword,
Into that strange vermilion ore running

Under the earth, following the shadows,
The beasts, the hunters of angels,

Toward some dark and liquid order,
I awake, a sergeant, a reptile,

Strumpet of hope, a pilgrim of fire.
Wings heavy, unseen, and hovering about my ear

Gather in the silence with a dark smell.
There is a river bent with mirrors,

Full of souls, curving their way
Toward the surface. A rare bird

Brings in the lighting
Like light on aluminum under water,

A smoky testament of silver,
Alabaster of alien desire. I remember

Drifting by on a barge with ancient books
Headed for open waters

Before the burning of the library at Abydos and Thebes.
I caught the swollen locket of one of my lives

Pinched on both ends by death, by breath,
By veiling that makes everything forgotten.

My eyes were closed for ten thousand days.
Gently, weirdly, like a surgeon

Opening the broken organs of his own brother,
I groped in the dark

For the hidden star in the skull.
Here the doorway, the movable key,

The impracticable logic, the stone- bound dialogue
Where the Gods who dream

Into bone and marble
At the boot end of imagination

Summon up the coarse biography in my veins.
I have been forgiven by all the women

I have failed to love, been set free

To marry the moody ghost pulling me,

A suddenly aired fish, fierce and grinning,
Through the womb-door. Past the skull's gate,

Past the under-roots of trees,
Past the violence of buried arrows, past

The panic of orchids,
The predatory migrations of vultures and bats,

My hands fold into an anthracite fist
With coral signatures oozing out the fingernails.

I grab the sun of a rising new light,
Speak in all the languages of red and gold

Until it quiets down, genuflects,
Colonizes the day with morning.

On an island of smooth black stone I emerge,
Look upward and see

The sorcerer in the soul again leaving the body,
The hidden Redeemer in the necropolis.

O spirit in the heartbeat of the first plunging bird,
Green magician beneath the stamen in the rose,

Appetite of the hippo, agility of the fly,
Fierce will of the salmon returning to its origin waters;

Cold metal of the sky,
Blue fruit overripe, fallen out of sight,

Out of mind, out of the oral darkness of night;
Lesson to the Spanish after the Moorish wars,

Aqueduct of blood between the liver and the heart;
Inventor of wine, scribe of epistles,

Dealer in knives, scarves and purple onions
In the marketplaces of Cyprus, Kiev,

And Mohenjo-Daro;
Brooding aboriginal in the thorn and briar,

Intimate illuminator on the birthmark of a frog;
Fornicating dreamer of Pan,

Apricot smell, salt belly of the oyster,
Papyrus reed grower and gatherer in the Nile;

Tomb protector, temple of secrets,
Final lover of the hopeless, the weak, the deformed.

Incubus who flies after midnight
And dives into the dreams, the hips,

The wishes of women,
Succubus who sucks out the life force of men.

Identity behind the mask,
Maskmaker of the Ages, the galactic spaces,

Hidden oracle of the races leaving earth to man,
And the races that are still to come after;

Dark sister of injuries and disorders.
Worker in amethyst, malachite and schist,

Grain in the redwood, the cedar, even the pine,
Relentless multiplier in the sexual organ of boys.

Canal sweeper, boxcar of hobos,

Peerless pirouette in the balance of ballerinas,

Gorgeous harlot, breasts of temple dancers,
Passageway between the world

And more subtle orders.
O Magus of colors in the turning earth,

Insurgent green in the resurrected grass,
Blue savannah in the summer sky,

Rumors, russets and ruins in autumn,
White hypnotist of the winter ice.

Original Sibyl, slender apothecary,
Knower of the thousand unknown names of god.

Maker of the black rain, black roots in the forest,
Ritual destroyer of stalagmites and saints

In underground caves, in the grottos of Venice.
O believer in rainbows, chromium and rice,

Idol of the prophets, idyll of the tides,
Source of the constant appetite of the worm and spider;

You are the Great Attractor drawing the receding constellations.
It is you in the orange rind I worship with my tongue.

It is you in the smell of new women, new harbors, new lawns.
It is you in the light-blood of the messenger angel,

You in the firing of a neuron, the collapse of a star.
Strength of the whale, sprinter between the planets,

Message in the wind above the undulating tidal grass;
Appeaser of the jackal, hollow eyes of the mummy,

Faith of the acolyte alone, at night,
In the middle of the desert.

Teacher of prayer, radiance and deliverance,
Teacher of the firefly, resolve of the stone,

Border between the air and a cast-off feather,
Arch in a willow bending toward the ground.

Wonder in the thunderstorm, sudden movement in the thicket,
Sudden outbreak of beauty

In the laws of a smile;
Sweet wonder in the chest of an aging priest

Stumbling into beauty and ecstasy at death.
Medicine of the enemy, medicine of the alchemists,

Medicine of the perfected Ones mastering the air
Who move beyond the circuitries of mercury and gold.

Pundit in the pepper root, white tongue of every flame,
Warm belly of women in orgasm with eyes of jade.

Sweet spot on the surface of strawberries,
Slippery rock in the throat of streams,

Bargainer at death's door, appeal of the serpents,
Secret tyranny of radios, banks and clocks.

O eloquent uterus of shadows and souls,
Highway gathering strength to the Afterlife,

Loops in the Hereafter, adventurer in light;
O gateway of the lucid and eternal return.

O writer of poetry to the animals and fish,

Vernal hero of all my days,

Witness of my folly, focus of my soul,
Illimitable benefactor of my blood

Moving in pathways yet to unfold.
O obsidian evangelist of the night sky,

I beseech you from the spent furnace of my will,
Accept my praise of your astounding art,

Wash me with Olokun into your eternal waters.

Glossary

Abydos (Abdju). One of the oldest cities of ancient Egypt/ Kemet. Located in Upper Egypt. It was the gateway to ancient nearly forgotten Nubia and the site of many temples. It was the place of the royal necropolis of the early pharaohs, including Seti 1 and Ramesses II. Site of many mysterious hieroglyphs and obscure rites of the old religion.

Duat (Tuat). The Kemetic Egyptian underworld where the soul went after death. The disembodied soul encounters here many mysterious, luminous and also frightening images and creatures before being judged. With discipline and good ethics while alive one's soul passed the test of the 'weighing of the heart' .It then passed on to the realm of the blessed. The Duat had/has a counterpart in the solar realm also. It is the home of Osiris(Ausar), Anubis, Thoth, Horus (Heru), Hathor and Ra. Often referenced in *The Book of the Dead, Pyramid texts, Coffin texts* etc. Its parallel can be seen in the *Tibetan Book of the Dead* as the Bardo Throdol.

Horus (Heru).Ancient Egyptian god. Celestial falcon and solar deity with pre-dynastic roots. This sky or solar deity was married to Hathor and eventually the opponent of Set. He was Son of Ra (Re) and later son of Osiris. Protector and patron of the pharaohs with many sites throughout Egypt sacred to him.

Nagas. Sanskrit for serpent, especially cobras. Semi-divine beings thought to be half serpent, half human. They live under-ground in great palaces called Naga-loka and are associated with waters, rivers, seas and are the guardians of treasure and advanced wisdom. They are the race of wise serpent beings that appear throughout world mythology and religion. "Be yea wise as serpents, harmless as doves"

Obatala. Youruba sky and creator god. In many traditions he is father of the Orisha, patron of peace, purity and mercy. Often seen as a noble older male dressed in white. Not to be confused with Olodumare the god of creation.

Olokun (Olocun) Yoruba god of the sea who lives in its depths. Known to be an aspect of Yemaya who is female.

Omphalos (Benben) Stone. Represents the primeval hill in many ancient religious and mythological systems where life emerged into our dimension. It is closely allied with the tree of Life, the World tree and axis mundi, the spine of the earth.

Ori. The head. The organic seat of the soul in West African Yoruba psycho-religious systems. It has disciplines associated with its awakening based on rhythm,devotion and sacrifice.

Orion. Prominent constellation on the celestial equator and visible throughout the earth. Brightest stars are Rigel and Betelgeuse. It rises *before* the star Sirius, the star whose heliacal rising was the basis for the accurate solar calendar of ancient Kemetic Egypt. It was a central star in all ancient world religions and mythologies.

Orisha. Emissaries of the high god in Yoruba religion. They are many and both rule over the forces of nature and also are *manifestations* of the different forms of the supreme god. Obatala is the elder most god.

Thoth (Tehuti).The ancient god of Egypt who was the patron of writing, scribes, science, wisdom, magic and both civil and religious practices. He recorded the final verdict of the heart in the afterlife in the great hall of Maat for all souls who passed through its gates into the underworld. Thus

the "God of Equilibrium" and "Master of Balance". He was believed to be the author of the "*Book of the Dead*". Often depicted as a man holding a scale or scrolls with the head of an ibis bird or baboon.

Ra (Re). Egyptian god of the sun and creator god who travelled across the earth daily in his solar bark, sailed into the underworld at night and re-emerged reborn each day. He rose from the ocean of chaos on the primeval hill and then created the eight other gods of ancient Egypt. Father of Heru/Horus.

About the Author

Edward Bruce Bynum is the author of several books of poetry and the winner of the national Naomi Long Madgett Poetry Prize for *Chronicles of the Pig & Other Delusions*. He is a clinical psychologist, author of several books in psychology, including *The Dreamlife of Families*, *DARK LIGHT CONSCIOUSNESS* and *The Roots of Transcendence*. He is a recipient of the Abraham H. Maslow award from the American Psychological Association. He lives in the Amherst Massachusetts area.